GLORY TO GOD IN THE HIGHEST

AND PEACE TO HIS PEOPLE ON EARTH

Glory © Mary Fleeson / www.lindisfarne-scriptorium.co.uk 2014

Glory

God's desire for us is to enjoy peace in this world, we weren't saved or create
ignore, oppress, war against or fear our neighbours. We are born with the abil
love unconditionally, without judgement or prejudice but we very quickly learn
seems worthy of our love and only rarely is the love we offer beyond our family
unconditional.

The English language has only one word for love but there are several l
mentioned in the Bible, the one that is perhaps the most important for us to pra
is Agape love, the ultimate, pure, unconditional, sacrificial, 'can only be done
God's help', 'die for someone', love.

Jesus said, "love one another. As I have loved you,". If we all did that in Agape
then peace, justice and true equality would follow. It seems like an unattair
dream but we have to be willing to try if only in our small corner of the world.

The angels singing their praises remind us that offering to God our Agape wor
restoring the wonder, majesty and glory of the Godhead, is part of achievin
goal of peace.

Teach Me

The words of the Psalmist are just as relevant today if we are to grow as hur
into our full potential and if we are to grow as Christians in a secular so
The Bible is our first resource for instructions on how to live but eve
Christendom interpretation differs and conflicts at times so how do we know wr
follow?

We can look at the life and teachings of Jesus, a man who gave his life becaus
trusted that God knew what He was doing. He had faith and he loved enough
for humanity. We can only aspire to do the same.

Holy Night

This Christmas piece was inspired by one of my favourite carols, 'O Holy Ni
The line I love the most is 'Fall on your knees! Oh, hear the angel voices!'
I imagine how the shepherds must have felt that night as they hurried to find
baby, presumably leaving their flocks for a while. Can you imagine how they r
have been brimming with anticipation? First they were 'terrified' by the appear
of the angels then they meet the newly born, longed for Messiah. Did they fe
their knees in awe? I would.
Try to spend some time in awe of what the birth of that tiny baby still means to
world. His message of love is no less powerful, radical and challenging than it
two thousand years ago. Fall on your knees…

Emmanuel

In this piece I have included the Romanised version of the word Emmanuel o
translation 'God with us' in many different alphabets to show that God came to e
and remains in the form of the Spirit, for everyone, regardless of race. We ar
God's children and loved equally and beyond measure.

The Star © Mary Fleeson / www.lindisfarne-scriptorium.co.uk 2014

The Star

Magi from the east came to Jerusalem and asked, "Where is the one who has b
born king of the Jews? We saw his star when it rose and have come to worship h
(Matthew 2:1-2)

Look into a clear night sky and try to count the stars, it's pretty impossible isn
Rather like trying to count the hairs on your head! But Jesus said that God kn
how many hairs each one of us has, we are so precious to God that each ha
counted, our creator God knows us intimately and cares about every part.

'Indeed, the very hairs of your head are all numbered.' (Luke 12:7)

The star that the Magi followed was one star amongst many and yet it told the s
of a new King. You are like that star, one of many humans on this planet but you
story can shine with Gods presence. The hairs on your head are counted, you
precious. Tell the stories of the King!

(continued on reverse of next imag

We Saw © Mary Fleeson / www.lindisfarne-scriptorium.co.uk 2014

We Saw

...Tell the stories of the King!

Imagination is often lacking in modern Christianity. In the days before the gen populace could read imagery provided an insight into Faith and those images, c illustrations in Bibles, were imagined by the artist who would have studied the V intimately. Today we read and we study, we question and dissect until imagina is pushed to the side in favour of fact and evidence but what if God wanted tc you more? If what He wanted to tell you was beyond words and beyond knowledge?

Try imagining yourself as a traveller two thousand years ago, you meet some who are following a star, you join them in their travels...

Retell the story of the Wise Men in your own words.

Read the beautifully imagined story of The Other Wise Man by Henry Van Dyke

My God I give to You this day,
Each word I think and say and pray,
Each action and each small step on the way,
I give my life to You this day.

This Day

The prayer in this piece, inspired by an old children's prayer, could be used e
day but the thinking behind it is as a prayer to say on each day of Lent. The
before Easter is a chance to prepare for the revelation of new Life. We may
time to consider that victory of life over death, what it means to truly die to self
what difference it makes to the everyday activity of living here in the world.

The blossom flowers, growing from what appears to be the dead branches
desolate tree, neatly symbolise life persisting in the face of death as we
reminded every Spring when the seemingly barren begins to live again.

A new command I give you: love one another

New Command

Sometimes it feels lonely in this big world and the injustices and cruelty that seem to flourish on our beautiful spinning planet make us question that promised love. God gave His beloved children freewill and with that a responsibility to show love in our actions. That wasn't a life tip just for Christians, it was a suggestion everyone. Some awful things happen in life, some of them can't be avoided but can do our best to counteract the deliberate wrongs in the world by doing as Jesus taught: 'You must love each other, just as I have loved you.' (John 13:34)

I Am © Mary Fleeson / www.lindisfarne-scriptorium.co.uk 2014

I Am

Jesus said to her, "I am the resurrection and the life. The one who believes in me will
live, even though they die; and whoever lives by believing in me will never die."
(John 11. 25-26)

There's a great bit of dry humour in this chapter in John about Lazarus, Jesus has
told the Disciples that he wants to return to Judea where the Jews wanted to stone
him, Jesus is adamant and Thomas says resignedly to the other Disciples "Let us
also go, that we may die with him."

It's a line worthy of any humourist, he didn't say 'we really shouldn't go, we could
die!' or even 'you know guys, this might be our last journey.' No, he made a flippant
comment that was important enough to include in the Gospel. Why? Perhaps it was
to show the camaraderie between the Disciples, they lived a precarious life in
community with each other, and without humour, community living is unbearable.

Spend some time dwelling on the funny side of life, what makes you laugh?

The Cross © Mary Fleeson / www.lindisfarne-scriptorium.co.uk 2014

The Cross

'He himself bore our sins' in his body on the cross, so that we might die to sins
live for righteousness; by his wounds you have been healed.' (1 Peter 2:24)

The empty cross is a symbol of hope, reminding us of the death and resurrectic
Jesus and the promise of eternal life to those who follow him, it is also a remind
the sacrifice that Jesus and his heavenly Father made.

'He is not here; he has risen!' (Luke 24:6)

Think about the empty cross and what it means to you.

JESUS REMEMBER ME WHEN YOU COME INTO YOUR KINGDOM

Kingdom © Mary Fleeson / www.lindisfarne-scriptorium.co.uk 2014

Kingdom

...'you will receive power when the Holy Spirit has come upon you; and you w
my witnesses in Jerusalem, in all Judea and Samaria, and to the ends of the e
When he had said this, as they were watching, he was lifted up, and a cloud
him out of their sight. (Acts 1:8-9)

Eyewitness accounts testify to both the empty tomb and Jesus' ascensio
heaven, today we don't have the luxury of having actually been there so we
our way of life on faith. We have faith because we know the man Jesus was
there is non-biblical evidence for this; we know that His teaching inspired r
thousands in the first century to give their lives to defend it and we can see pro
our faith in the answered prayers and miracles that continue to happen today.

If you declare with your mouth, "Jesus is Lord," and believe in your heart that
raised him from the dead, you will be saved. (Romans 10:9)

Christus Resurrexit

Resurrexit

While he was going and they were gazing up towards heaven, suddenly two me
white robes stood by them. They said, 'Men of Galilee, why do you stand lookin
towards heaven? This Jesus, who has been taken up from you into heaven
come in the same way as you saw him go into heaven. (Acts 1:9-11)

"Christ is risen!"

From the tomb and to the Father, Jesus' Resurrection and Ascension defies lo
explanation, to some it puts doubt on the validity of Christianity alongside the \
birth, the Transfiguration and the Miracles but when we choose to believe be
what we know perhaps we can begin to understand a limitless God. Why sh
God have the boundaries we humans have?

Then Jesus told him, "...blessed are those who have not seen and yet
believed." (John 20:29)

Flames © Mary Fleeson / www.lindisfarne-scriptorium.co.uk 2014

Flames

'When the day of Pentecost came, they were all together in one place. Sudde[n]
sound like the blowing of a violent wind came from heaven and filled the w[hole]
house where they were sitting. They saw what seemed to be tongues of fire[that]
separated and came to rest on each of them. All of them were filled with the [Holy]
Spirit,' (Acts 2:1-4)

Flames have represented Gods presence on other occasions, most notably i[n the]
book of Exodus as the burning bush and the pillar of fire. To humanity fire[is a]
symbol of light, warmth, danger and destruction, God is also those things.

The Spirit of God is within you and around you, the 'tongues of fire' that inspire[d the]
disciples to go out and tell the world about Jesus are waiting to be released i[n you]
and from you, will you accept the challenge?

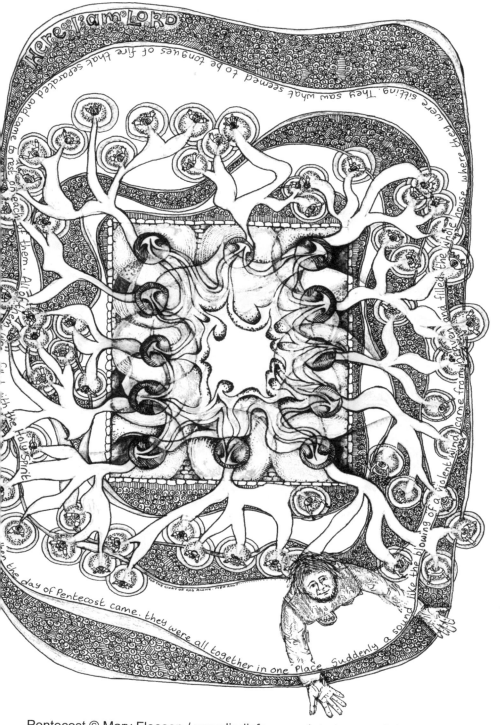

Pentecost

From the central flame each disciple within the room is touched and the flame
Spirit continues to change lives as they begin their mission. Each figure and
represents another life changed, their arms are open wide in expectation
acceptance.

Are you open to receive the Spirit?

Sow and Reap

"Others, like seed sown on good soil, hear the word, accept it, and produce a
thirty, sixty or even a hundred times what was sown."

'Sow and Reap' shows the sower scattering seeds and a tree in full fruit, bot
included because you simply can't have a harvest without having prepared the
planted the seeds and nurtured them. It is an analogy for life that Jesus us
good effect in the Parable of the Sower (Matthew 13 v3-20).

How can we nurture people? We need more than just food and water alth
without those things we would die. Jesus answered the tempter in the desert,
shall not live on bread alone, but on every word that comes from the mouth of
(Matthew 4:4 and Deuteronomy 8:3)

'Every word that comes from the mouth of God'... the 'word' is the breath of
that divine blessing that marks each of us as a child of God. Our purpose is to
everyone to recognise their inheritance and to fulfil their potential through love

Yet to all who did receive him, to those who believed in his name, he gave the
to become children of God – children born not of natural descent, nor of h
decision or a husband's will, but born of God. (John1 12-13)

Wheat © Mary Fleeson / www.lindisfarne-scriptorium.co.uk 2014

Wheat

What does Harvest mean to the average person on the street?

It used to be a time for giving thanks for the food produced because life
precarious and a good harvest could easily mean the difference between lif
death for the following year. Now, in the Western world we have c
supermarkets, vegetables from the other side of the world and enough surplu
to eradicate hunger completely if other factors weren't an issue.

Today celebrating a festival isn't enough, we do need to celebrate and give t
for what we have but it mustn't stop there, as well-fed consumers we need
difficult questions about why people are starving and why poverty continues.